FEB   2011

DATE DUE

ANIMAL PREDATORS
Crocodiles

SANDRA MARKLE

❦ CAROLRHODA BOOKS, INC. / MINNEAPOLIS

THE ANIMAL WORLD IS FULL OF
PREDATORS.

Predators are the hunters who find, catch, and eat other animals—their prey—in order to survive. Every environment has its chain of hunters. The smaller, slower, less able predators become prey for the bigger, faster, more cunning hunters. And everywhere, there are just a few kinds of predators at the top of the food chain. *Along the Nile River in Africa, one of these is the crocodile.*

After developing for nearly three months, this little male is hatching. He yelps and bumps his egg tooth, the hard lumplike scale on the end of his nose, against the inside of the shell until he breaks out. The other babies are hatching too, and mother crocodile hears their calls. She claws aside the dirt that covers their nest. Then she scoops up the newly hatched young in her mouth. Although her jaws are strong enough to crush bone, the mother gently carries her offspring to a nearby inlet of the Nile River. This will be their nursery while they grow bigger. In the beginning, a baby crocodile is as small as a baby chicken, but it increases almost 4,000 times in size as it grows up.

One day this little male may be about 16 feet long (about 5 meters long)—about the length of an average-sized car—and feed on prey such as zebras and wildebeest. But he's got a lot of growing to do before he's ready to tackle such big prey.

Still, from the time he hatches the little male has to catch his own meals. His body is designed to make him a successful hunter. Ears that open through slits behind his eyes let him hear the dragonfly even before he sees it. When the insect is overhead, the crocodile's big eyes let him judge how far to lunge. With a sudden sweep of his tail, the little crocodile surges upward as he opens his jaws wide.

When the little crocodile strikes, his jaws snap together, crushing the dragonfly. The muscles that close his mouth are much stronger than the ones that open it. That's important because a crocodile's main weapons are its tooth-edged jaws.

Crocodiles may see prey and then slip up on it to attack. But crocodiles usually hunt by waiting and suddenly attacking prey that comes within range. So the little crocodile floats under the water with only his eyes and nostrils poking through the surface. Suddenly, special sensors on the sides of his jaws let the little hunter "feel" a fish approaching. When he senses the fish is close enough to strike, the little crocodile lunges and snaps, catching a fish dinner.

For the first few months of the young crocodile's life, he spends most of his time among the reeds in the little inlet. He is hiding from predators such as mongooses and wading birds. When his mother returns to the nursery between hunts, the little male feels safe enough to bask in the sun. Crocodiles do not produce body heat, so he needs to soak up heat from the world around him to be warm enough to be active and digest his food. Because he doesn't have to use food energy to produce body heat, though, much of that food energy goes to making him grow bigger.

Gaining about 1 foot (30 centimeters) in length each year, the young male is soon too big to be prey for most predators. About the only predator he has to watch out for is a bigger crocodile. When prey is plentiful, the young male hunts in the same area with other crocodiles about his size. When he isn't hunting, he often waddles ashore to rest alongside them. That way many eyes and ears can check for danger. When the young male sees other youngsters heading for the water, he doesn't take time to find out what the trouble is. He hurries into the water too and swims away.

The young crocodile often stays close to other young crocodiles at night too. They find safety in numbers. The young male also hunts at night. In the dark, it's harder for his prey to spot him lurking in the water, but he can see them even in dim light. His pupils, the openings that let light enter his eyes, are able to open extra wide. This lets as much light as possible reach the retina, the light-sensitive layer at the back of each eye. The crocodile's eyes seem to glow because there is a mirrorlike layer, called the *tapetum lucidum,* behind the retina. This layer bounces light back to the retina, increasing the amount of light it receives.

As the male grows bigger, he spends more time hunting and resting alone. He begins to hunt regularly in one area, his hunting territory. He usually rests in the same place on the river's bank too, basking in the sun. As the day warms up, the crocodile warms up too. When he is too warm, he opens his big jaws to let the air evaporate moisture from the inside of his mouth. That cools him off.

When the crocodile can't cool off enough, he waddles into the river until only his big head is on the surface. There he waits for prey to come to the river. Finally, as the day fades and a breeze wafts across the water, the crocodile catches the scent of a gazelle. Behind the crocodile's nostrils are canals as long as his snout. Because these long canals are packed with chemical-sensitive cells, the crocodile has a keen sense of smell. So the crocodile follows his nose to find the prey.

By the time the gazelle herd reaches the riverbank, the crocodile is within striking range. He dives underwater. A chemical in his body slows his heartbeat and shifts blood from his lungs to the rest of his body. Flaps of skin seal his ears, his nostrils, and the back of his throat. This way, the crocodile can hold his breath for more than an hour. Semitransparent eyelids slide over his eyes like goggles. He can't see as well, but that doesn't matter. Under the water, he surges straight toward the point where he last saw his prey. Then he surfaces and lunges, catching the gazelle in his big jaws. Next, the crocodile dives again, holding the gazelle underwater until it drowns.

Since all of the crocodile's teeth are sharp for biting, he isn't able to chew or grind up his food, as other animals do. To eat his prey, the crocodile holds the gazelle in his jaws, lifts the animal out of the water, and violently slings it to one side. The weight of the gazelle's body tears the rest of it away from the part the crocodile is holding. Then the male lifts his nose and tosses the torn-off part down his throat. Because his tongue is attached to the floor of his mouth, this is the only way he can swallow. Ready for more, the crocodile locates what's left of his prey and repeats the bite, swing, and gulp process.

With a stomach about the size of a basketball, the crocodile is soon full. He crawls out onto a warm sandbar to rest and soak up the heat he needs to digest his food. The crocodile lost a tooth in this attack, but a replacement will soon move up from inside his jaw to fill the space. Because the crocodile regularly loses and replaces teeth, his jaws are armed with teeth of many different sizes.

By the time the crocodile is ten years old, he is about 12 feet long (nearly 4 m). He is one of the biggest predators on the Nile River.

Plant-eating grazing animals, such as zebras, must come to the Nile River to get the fresh water they need. But getting a drink can be dangerous. In the river, crocodiles have the advantage because they are such good swimmers. By going to the river as part of a herd, or large group, the grazers have lots of help watching for crocodiles. Zebras' eyes are high on their heads so they can watch for approaching crocodiles even while getting a drink.

Out on the sandbar, the big male crocodile spots the zebra herd approaching
the river. He watches until he sees one zebra walk
away from the herd into deeper water. Then
he slides into the water and swims so
slowly there is barely a ripple.

Before the hunter reaches striking range, though, one member of the herd spots the crocodile and calls out an alarm. Immediately, the zebra herd backs away from the river. The crocodile surges forward to attack. He digs in with his long claws and quickly climbs up the riverbank. But the zebra bounds out of the water even faster. And once on land, the zebra has the advantage because it can run faster than the crocodile.

Several days pass before the big crocodile has another chance to get close enough to a prey animal to attack. Then, as the last of the day's heat shimmers above the cool water, the crocodile sees a herd of wildebeest approach the river. The herd hesitates on the bank, looking and sniffing the air. They're checking for crocodiles. But the big male is almost completely underwater. The wildebeest don't see him or smell him. Finally, thirst drives the wildebeest herd into the water to drink.

The crocodile very slowly swims closer until he's near enough to strike.
As the big male explodes from the water, he opens his jaws wide.

Snorting in panic, the wildebeest leap to get out of the crocodile's way. The big male's jaws snap shut on a calf's leg. Bawling with fear, the calf struggles to escape. The big hunter opens his jaws to bite again, and the calf bounds ashore to safety.

The wildebeest snort and grunt in panic. Those closest to the water kick and leap, struggling to bound away as the hunter attacks again. This time, the crocodile's jaws clamp shut on an adult wildebeest. The crocodile backs into the river, dragging his prey underwater. Within minutes the wildebeest is dead. Then the crocodile eats his fill. The big male has more food than he needs, so he dives underwater with the leftovers. He stores these for later by wedging them into a hollow between two large rocks.

Crocodiles can survive as long as one year without eating, but they prefer to eat often. So after the wildebeest hunt, the big crocodile watches as a bird searching for food along the riverbank comes closer, step by step. Finally, the bird is so close the crocodile can't resist grabbing a snack. He lunges and swallows the bird in one gulp. Satisfied for the moment, the big male falls asleep on the sunny riverbank.

Several days pass before the crocodile has a chance to eat again. A gazelle's alarm call alerts the big crocodile. Another male has just caught a gazelle and is pulling it into deeper water. As that hunter dives underwater with its prey, the big male waddles into the river.

As the biggest crocodile on this part of the Nile, the big male swims over to claim a share of the kill. The smaller crocodile lets him take it. Crocodiles don't usually fight over prey. In the crocodile world, bigger crocodiles have more power than smaller ones.

The big male needs food energy for more than growth. It is nearly time to mate.

The rainy season triggers chemical changes in both male and female crocodiles. The big male patrols his territory and drives away rival males. When a female enters, though, he lets her swim close enough to bump against him. He responds by pushing her and making a purring sound. After a while, the pair mate. Then the female goes on her way. In about a month, she will lay eggs to produce a new batch of young hunters.

Many years in the future, one of these young may replace the big male as the top predator on his part of the Nile River.

Looking Back

- Take a close look at the crocodile on page 3 to check out its scaly skin. These tough scales have stretchy skin in between to allow the crocodile to twist and bend. Some of the scales on the crocodile's back have bony plates to create a tough armor.

- Take another look at the crocodile eating on page 18. Crocodiles also swallow pebbles or gravel. Some researchers think these help grind up the food. Others think the weight of the stones help the crocodile stay at the river bottom. What do you think?

- A walking crocodile, like the one on page 23, can push its belly off the ground to move faster. If it's chasing prey, the crocodile can even gallop as fast as 11 miles per hour for about 50 feet (18 kilometers per hour for 15 m).

Glossary

EGG TOOTH: a small, bumplike scale on the baby crocodile's nose that it uses to break out of its egg. The crocodile later sheds this scale.

GAZELLE: a small, fast antelope that lives in Africa and Asia

HERD: a group of the same kind of animal, which feeds and travels together

NEST: a hole the female crocodile digs into the sandy dirt into which she lays eggs. She then covers the eggs with dirt.

NILE RIVER: a river in northeastern Africa that is the longest river in the world

NOSTRILS: twin openings on the top of the crocodile's nose. The nostrils can close to keep water from getting into the crocodile's lungs when it dives.

PREDATOR: an animal that is a hunter

PREY: an animal that a predator catches to eat

RETINA: the light-sensitive layer at the back of each of the crocodile's eyes

TERRITORY: the section of the river and nearby riverbank where the crocodile usually hunts.

TONGUE: a special muscle attached to the floor of the mouth that has a flap at the back to help seal off the throat when the crocodile dives underwater

WILDEBEEST: a large African antelope that grazes in large herds. When they drink at the Nile River, they become one of the crocodile's main food sources.

ZEBRA: black-and-white striped grazing animal that looks similar to a horse

Further Information

Books

Simon, Seymour. *Crocodiles and Alligators.* New York: Harper Trophy, 2001. This book has fascinating facts and ancient lore about these animals and information on how they are making a comeback.

Sloan, Chris. *Super Croc and Other Prehistoric Crocodiles.* Washington, D. C.: National Geographic, 2002. The book follows Dr. Paul Sereno's expedition to locate Super Croc, the fossilized remains of a supersized crocodile. The book also traces the development of today's crocodiles and their kin.

Walker, Sally. *Crocodiles.* Minneapolis: Carolrhoda Books, Inc., 2004. Photographs and text describe the life cycle of the crocodile.

Wexo, John Bonnett. *Alligators & Crocodiles.* San Diego, CA: Zoobooks/Wildlife Education, 2000. This book is packed with facts about the animals and their home environments.

Videos

National Geographic's Crocodiles: Here Be Dragons (National Geographic, 1990.) Dramatic footage shows these animals hunting. It also shows how as many as 90 percent of the young crocodiles that hatch each year fall prey to other animals.

National Geographic's Last Feast of the Crocodiles (National Geographic, 1996.) This video shows crocodiles surviving a serious drought.

Predators of the Wild: Crocodiles & Alligators (Warner Home Video, 1993.) This video shows how these animals catch prey and raise their young in the wild.

Index

With love for Marcia Marshall, in appreciation for all her help and encouragement

The author would like to thank Kent A. Vliet, crocodilian biologist at the University of Florida, Department of Zoology, for sharing his expertise and enthusiasm. As always, a special thanks to Skip Jeffery, for his help and support.

Photo Acknowledgments
© Nigel J. Dennis; Gallo Images/CORBIS, p. 1; © Frans Lanting/Minden Pictures, pp. 3, 4, 9, 12, 15, 21, 22, 36; © Mark Deeble and Victoria Stone/Oxford Scientific Films, pp. 6, 7, 8, 18, 27, 28, 29, 30; © Joe McDonald, p. 11; © Mitsuaki Iwago/Minden Pictures, p. 14; © Mike Powles/Oxford Scientific Films, p. 16; © Peter Johnson/ CORBIS, p. 23; © A&M Shah/Animals Animals, pp. 24, 34; © Joe McDonald/Bruce Coleman, Inc., p. 33; © Fritz Polking/Bruce Coleman, Inc., p. 35; © Erwin and Peggy Bauer, p. 37.
Cover: © Shah Manoj/Animals Animals.
Back cover: © Frans Lanting/Minden Pictures.

Carolrhoda Books, Inc.
A division of Lerner Publishing Group
241 First Avenue North
Minneapolis, MN 55401

Website address: www.lernerbooks.com

Library of Congress Cataloging-in-Publication Data

Markle, Sandra.
    Crocodiles / by Sandra Markle.
      p. cm. — (Animal predators)
    Summary: Discusses the lives of crocodiles, focusing on how they hunt their prey.
    Includes bibliographical references and index.
    ISBN: 1—57505—726—3 (lib. bdg. : alk. paper)
    ISBN: 1—57505—742—5 (pbk. : alk. paper)
    1. Crocodiles—Juvenile literature. [1. Crocodiles.] I. Title. II. Series.
  QL666.C925M374 2004
  597.98'2—dc22   2003015402

Manufactured in the United States of America
1 2 3 4 5 6 — DP — 09 08 07 06 05 04